How to Create Demand for Your Service: Limit the Supply and the Value Goes Up

Category: Business & Economics

Author: Bob Oros

Publisher: Bob Oros Publishing

ISBN: 978-1-387-20113-6

Copyright 2017

I0475157

Description: If there is an unlimited supply your product becomes a commodity. Limit the supply, the demand increases and the value goes up. A restaurant always had a line waiting to get in to eat. When asked why he didn't expand his seating, he said that waiting in line was part of the mystique of eating at his establishment and if that changed, he might lose business. If people think a place is worth waiting in line for, it must be great.

Key words: sales techniques, job in sales, sales manager training, manufacturing sales training, wholesale sales training, distributor sales training, food service sales, sales coaching, motivating sales people, sales course, online sales training, food sales jobs,

ISBN 978-1-387-20113-6

1. Create demand for your product or service.

When I lived in Orlando, Florida, the visionary Walt Disney had a team of folks buy all the property he needed to build Disney World. They were able to keep everyone sworn to secrecy. As soon as the purchase became known and everyone found out what was going on, the property values went sky high. We are living in a new age with a new kind of ownership, but the principles stay the same. I have been secretly buying a series of internet properties and I am now the largest dot com property owner in the More Success category on the internet.

How much are all those "properties" worth? That is an interesting question. The answer can be found by using a comparison. If you wanted to sell hot dogs in New York City you would have to buy a license. There are only a certain number of licenses available, which makes them increase in value. The current selling price for a hot dog cart license in New York City is between $350,000 and $500,000.

The same is true for a taxi cab license.

Wallstreet.com sold for one million dollars. Business.com sold for seven million dollars. The Los Angles Country Club was built in the 1950's at which time you could buy one of a thousand available memberships for $5,000. The standing price today is one million dollars.

You can see that people want what they can't have. When they can't have it, value is created.

How can this help you?

Here is an example.

There is a Martial Arts company near my home and my nephew is a member. When he first started going he was getting a lot of individual attention. Being a member of the team was important. After a year things started to change. The instructor wanted to go form 50 students to 150 students. He moved to a more expensive location, hired some help, and now spends most of his time chasing after new recruits to help pay for his increased overhead. He is actually making less money than he was with his original 50, many whom have left.

What if he understood the concept of supply and demand?

What if he would have raised his price and limited his students to 50. The only way you could become a member would be by referral and then you had to fill out an application and go through an interview process along with the parents. Interviews would be held only once per month on the second Tuesday from noon until 9:00 PM, by appointment. What if, rather than answer his phone you heard a recording that said he was training his students and is unable to come to the phone because he didn't want to interrupt their focus and concentration. What if all phone calls were returned at the end of the day by his wife (who works with him as his office assistant) and finds out what they wanted. If it was important enough, a phone appointment would be set up with the instructor.

This is the same strategy doctors and dentists use to create a sense of being busy. They schedule appointment times close together and make you wait.

When you are talking with a prospect and you have made the call on them, imply that you are only there to see if they qualify for you to spend time and energy helping them solve their problems.

Here is another example.

Trade show attendance has always a problem with many companies. Some of the smart companies are only allowing people to attend who are purchasing a certain dollar volume from them. They have even required an RSVP with a deposit that is refundable towards the purchase of anything at the show.

This is the law of supply and demand. If there is an unlimited supply, you and your products become a commodity. However, if you can somehow limit the supply, the demand will not only increase, the value will go up as well.

Comments:

Back in the 1970's the Detroit auto makers decided to stop making convertibles because of the extra production cost and the sales not once they once were. The last production run for any manufacturer was the 1976 Cadillac Eldorado. When people found out that convertibles weren't being made anymore the demand went up for any convertible new or used[this really helped the collector car market]. After a few years the automakers realized that there was a good market for convertibles still and started making some models again [first one back was the 1984 Chrysler Lebaron]. So true people want what they can't have [I've managed not to sell my 1967 Buick GS400 convertible all these years because it is rare and a lot of people want it but it's better than money in the bank].

Cary McAfee

People, including our customers, want to do business with successful people. To a lot of them, busy is successful. I will rarely answer a customers' first attempt to contact me even if my phone isn't busy. I want them to know I'm busy and my time is valuable to them. I want them to know I am focused on the customer I am with or who's business I am taking care of at the moment. Sometimes I use that "lag time" to switch gears and focus on that customer who attempted to call me before I call them back. When I do return that call,(promptly) they know the time is theirs and that it is valuable.

Chris Chase

There is a restaurant I called on that always had a line waiting to get in to eat. When asked why he didn't expand his seating, he said that waiting in line was part of the mystique of eating at his establishment and if that changed, he might lose business. If people think that a place is worth waiting in line for, it must be great and the thing to do.

Larry Edmondson

Customers need to have their confidence built up about your product or service. I think using names of your satisfied customers that he knows, especially his competitors, is one of the most effective ways to do this. He does not want to be left behind his competitors when a good opportunity is available.

Crocker Smith

The example that was shown in the article was a medical office that makes sure their appointments are scheduled together so that the patients think the doctor is busy. I really agree with this. I have worked in a Chiropractic office before and it works.

You can also do the same in Staffing. In the past when making appointments with new clients I make sure that I am not available all the time. This gives the clients the impression that you are busy because other customers need your assistance too. "I am available Tuesday at 2:00pm and Thursday at 10:00am. Are either of those times good for you?"

If your business is in a small city you can also mention other clients that are very happy with your business. In the past I have carried a book around of client reference letters. It never hurts!

Danah Parmley

Supply and demand is basic in the business world. It is true, people want what other people have and then they really want it if they can't have it. So how can we make people want out service? We have to let them know that we are in high demand as are the people and services we supply. Will everyone jump on board, probably not but some will and that's all it takes to get the ball rolling.

Brandon Sanchez

Supply and demand is the very foundation of successful sales. People want what they can't have; it's a simple fact of life. And to make that statement even truer, people are willing to pay outrageous amounts to get it.

I fell victim to it. A golf course I played at decided it wanted to cut down on the crowding and went to a membership policy. A golf game went from $45 to $250 plus a $500 a month membership fee.

Matthew Thacker

"I've also noticed that, not only do people want what they can't have, but they want what other people want. I made a sales call to present our payroll service to a gentleman about a month and 1/2 ago. He was interested but never would commit. Yesterday I went to go visit him again to check in. He was still half interested half not really. When I told him that a company in the area, about his companies size, was astounded by the service we provide and can't wait to sign up he became a lot more interested."

Angie Dussouy

2. How can you use suggestion to increase your sales?

With a little "suggestive selling" you can easily put more money in your pocket. People tend to act in accordance with the ideas that are in their minds, and many of these ideas, in the form of suggestions, may be put there by you.

This being the case, you should look for every opportunity to make suggestions that will result in getting what you want. Selling through suggestion should be considered not only as a way to increase profits but also as a form of service to the buyer.

Suggestions bring to his or her attention items that might otherwise be overlooked. If suggestions are tactfully made, they impress the customer with our desire to be of service.

Make a habit of calling your customer's attention to new merchandise, to specials, to other items in connection with what they are already buying and you will be enhancing your relationship while increasing your business.

You should always be on the alert for the suggestion of things that will "go with" the merchandise you are selling. If you do not carry the exact item that the customer wants, you should, by all means, suggest a substitute.

Suggesting a higher quality product than the one they are buying may perform a real service. Most customers appreciate having their attention directed to new or unusual items. Every time something new comes on the market it opens an opportunity to make a suggestion to your customers.

You should be careful not to suggest anything that will cause the customer to act contrary to what you want.

This can be illustrated in the case of the sales person who followed the practice of telling customers that if they did not like the product he would be happy to issue a credit for it. The sales manager noticed that this sales person was giving out way too many credits and instructed him to stop suggesting the credit guarantee, even though the company would guarantee the product.

Once the sales person stopped making the suggestion – the credits stopped.

Comments:

Suggestive selling "farming, planting the seeds" truly is a cornerstone to selling. For a prospect, it could be just planting that 'seed of doubt' on their current supplier without placing the current supplier's name to your seed. For your customer, its building on the relationship, planting the seeds for future sales, offering products, ideas, knowledge, conversation. For you, it's the 'harvesting', taking ownership, building on your profits.

David Vize

A good technique is what I call "reverse suggestive selling" and usually is successful. When there is an opportunity to down-sell a customer, either to save him money or make his purchase more efficient, point it out. This quickly builds credibility and trust and lessens the natural anti-salesman defenses of the customer paving the way for future sales. The result will be even higher profits.

Crocker Smith

The first example of suggestive selling that comes to mind was recently used at a convenient store. I brought a pack of Lance peanut butter crackers to the cashier and she politely asked if I would like a bottle of water to go with my crackers. She did not know I already had a bottle of water in my car but that was a very observant and smart question to ask. Suggestive selling at its' best.

Gregg Nixon

Suggestive selling is something that many sales people shy away from doing. They feel like they are being way too pushy. My previous employer was an irrigation supply company that also sold direct shipments of plants. One of our best customers did not even know we sold plants because we all thought he knew and was simply buying his plants somewhere else. When he found out we sold plants he was upset with us for doing a disservice to his business. Luckily we kept his irrigation business and gained his plant business after a lot of convincing. He would have bought plants from the beginning from us if he had simply known about them. It is very important to show every customer ever product. You cannot take you customer's knowledge for granted.

Cullin Hamm

3. What do politicians and insurance companies talk about?

Politicians don't talk about needs, they talk about the future. Successful politicians use this concept of selling the future in every speech. They know that if they want to stay in office or be elected to office they have to know what the people want and build it in to every talk they give. They never like to talk about the past and very rarely address issues in the present, it's always the future. "I am your bridge to the 21st century". "Your door to the future".

A travel agent talks about a future trip that will give you a really good time. A travel agency always gives you a clear vision of where you are going, never on the trip getting there. A seven day cruise sales presentation shows you the fun you will have on board ship, all the food and entertainment you will enjoy. However, they neglect to tell you about the 7 hour flight to Puerto Rico where you meet the ship and the 4 hours you have to stand on the dock waiting in line.

Insurance companies talk about a future full of accidents, fires, floods, sickness, death and financial ruin. The insurance industries entire existence relies on selling you the future. When you buy insurance you spend thousands of dollars and have nothing in return except a piece of paper. They present you with a mental picture of what would happen to your family if you were to die. They show you how many people reach old age without any money or retirement. They give examples of the high cost of going to the hospital for surgery. The insurance companies are experts at getting a piece of your future. This does not mean that it is good or bad, it simply is the way they sell their products and services.

Lawyers talk about a future full of pain and suffering. A good lawyer is the true artist in the area of painting future pictures. They usually do it based on fear of loss. When you tell them about your concern they paint a picture of gloom by blowing your problem up to the maximum. Then, of course, they tell you how much work it would be to take care of it and, with no guarantees, will represent you for a fee.

Credit card companies talk about a future you don't have to wait for. One of the single largest goals of most people today is to have the money to pay off their credit card balances. How did so many people get in this situation where the average married couple owes around $25,000 in credit card bills. Once we look at the concept of appealing to someone's future, creating an impatience and a willingness to go in debt for things they didn't think they could live without, it is easy to understand why people borrow on their future. During the last 12 months over one million people filed personal bankruptcy to get out from under their debts.

Law enforcement talks about a future behind bars. Law enforcement is similar to the way the lawyers use this powerful concept. The worst thing that could happen to an individual is to have their future taken away from them. Every time we watch a movie where someone is put behind bars with no hope we can't help feel how that would be. If would be criminals knew for a fact that they would be caught there would be no crime. What a criminal sees is getting away with something unearned. Getting caught is hardly a possibility for them.

What do you talk to your customers about?

Price?

Features and benefits?

Or how your product or service can enhance their future?

Comments:

Insurance sales has to be the epitome of sales "combat". I've been approached several times throughout the last 3 decades by companies attempting to hire me to sell insurance. I honestly can't imagine selling a product where you have to drag up all the negative things that could happen to people if you DON'T buy a product, nor can I imagine selling an expensive, ongoing schedule of payments to a person who, in exchange, receives a piece of paper...TOUGH JOB! That being said I understand the need for it.

I feel blessed to be able to work in a sales profession that deals in tangibles as well as the future. Honestly though, it's the intangibles we look to service that set us apart as a company. Service, service, service and a partnership for positive growth with the accounts we work with.

Chris Chase

The past is done and is set in facts, the present is what we are "working" in now, the future is the only area that our mind allows us to paint the way we would want to see it. As a sales person, if you can take your products, services, and those benefits then tap into the "future" of your customer, you will have a sale.

David Vize

Talking to the customer about the future is very important. People live by planning for the future, so that would be a great sales approach! I care about the present, what's happening now, but I am constantly planning and headed toward the "future".

Brooke Knight

Not all companies have needs right now when we are in front of them. Some may and that's great but when that isn't the case we have to let them know they will have a need our services in the future. We also want to let them know we want to be the one they turn to when that need comes up. We can also tell them that our services and

prices can greatly impact the future of their business by offering outstanding service while helping them save money.

Brandon Sanchez

The majority of sales goes right along with selling the future. You could anything if you can tie it directly into a future with benefits. People want the future and work hard preparing and detailing every little part of it. Why, because people seem to rest easier when they think the future is planned for. If you can fit your product into that picture, you already have your foot in the door.

Matthew Thacker

Painting a pretty picture for the future is a great way to make a sale. Most companies focus on the future of the company rather than the present. When making a presentation I try to stay away from the price as long as I can. This is not because our prices are through the roof, because they are not. It I because I want my customers to appreciate what my services will do for their company before they even think about price. If you can achieve this, you may be able to sell your services at a slightly higher margin. If I can paint a pretty picture of the future my chances of making the sell increase dramatically.

Cullin Hamm

Great concept. Sell the future. We can still integrate this message without going completely away from current sales tactics. We should just weave in facts about how our "price" can benefit them "in the future", and how our "features and benefits" can be true "future" benefits for the client.

Scott Green

The future is of the utmost importance. This is a great concept to use when talking to customers. I try and tell them all the benefits our services would give them, but I believe I will start using the word "future" when I talk about the benefits and what our service can do for them. I probably have been referring to the future when I talk to customers, however, I do believe that word itself, FUTURE, will make an even greater impact on what they are hearing.

Patsy "CiCi" Clements

4. How can you put customers on a magic carpet?

This is the secret of a highly successful sales person. Your average sales person talks about the price, the competition or the product, always in the present tense. The consultative sales person looks at their product or service from a different view point.

The first question you should ask when putting together your sales strategy is: What does my prospect or customer want? What are the pictures they have of their future? What are their goals? Where do they want to be next year, the year after, and five years from now?

You have to go beyond the money and find out what they are going to do with it once they have it. Once you get this information you can move on to the next step in building your sales presentation.

The second question you ask is how can the benefits of my products and services enhance my clients' future? When we begin to think in these terms we have crossed the bridge from sales person to a true "Consultative Sales Person". Once you begin to think in these terms, your prospects turn into customers and your customers turn into clients. You have set yourself apart from the average "peddler" who merely has a sales pitch, and put yourself in the position of a partner who is working for the same goals and objectives as your client.

Your customers will know that you "understand where they are coming from." They will know that you understand their problems and have an insight into what they are trying to accomplish.

I spent 2 years living full time in an RV traveling throughout North America. I became hooked on stopping at RV dealers and talking with sales people. Most of them talked about the features of their products and very seldom about my traveling experiences and future dreams. They were simply tour guides pointing out the table and the stove.

However, every now and then I would come across a real pro who asked me questions about my future plans. What a treat it was to climb on the magic carpet and visit my future. Even though I no longer own an RV, it is still fun to get on that magic carpet and revisit the care free lifestyle.

Comments:

Being part of the here & now is fine if the service or product offered is beneficial to the customer at the present time, but to establish a long term partnership with the customer in the future is to look beyond the here & now. You have to be able to see their future & future goals & show how you can be a valued asset to their vision. Once you've accomplished that then you can become a partner instead of a one time sales person.

Carla McCrea

Gathering information on a prospect's wants, needs, short and long term goals are a perfect start to preparing the magic carpet. Customizing your presentation with emphasis on features or benefits you offer that can contribute to the success of the prospect. Think of yourself as a partner to their business instead of the sales representative.

Brooke Knight

A consultative sales person using the future is the best way to move forward with a customer.

James L. Craft, Jr.

With my portfolio of accounts, my biggest sales pitch for the end user customer is how being compliant with what their head office puts into place will help them in the future. The local operators tend to be in the "now" frame of mind, whereas the head office is in the "future" frame of mind. Supporting the head office, and helping the stores to become compliant about "showing" them the future is the key aspect to my line of selling.

JoAnne Welch

"I have found that it seems to depend on the customer. Some customers have no idea, at least it seems that way, of where they want to be next week let alone in five years. They seem to be only interested in the here and now. After thinking about this statement perhaps...

1 They are not the type of customer that I would want or...

2 Perhaps they have never been shown the future so it would be up to me to take them for a tour to see if I can take them to the next level ??"

Alex McQueen

"This was the lesson I was looking for--re the consultative sale. It's going to help me a lot becuase it will require replanned and thought out benefits before I talk to the next prospect. Very helpful!"

Mike Rohan

"This is the whole idea of selling. "

Ronda Kennesaw

"In the staffing business I have learned that we play a vital role in our company's future goals. Helping them achieve these goals becomes as important to us as it is to them. The more they thrive and grow the bigger the role we will play. Our survival depends on how we assist our clients with their future goals and concerns. I believe that we do this through our ability to be flexible. If it is possible we try to meet all of our different clients needs on an individual level. If a client needs something done differently we can tailor our business model to their desires along as we do not jeopardize integrity and go beyond the boundsries set forth by the corporate office. I would like to think we are fast, fluid and flexible."

Jeffrey Mole

"In order to sell a product or service you must be able to show how it will improve their business. The most effective way to do this is to find out exactly what the customer's ambitions are and how he plans to implement these ambitions. If you can show how your product or service can improve their goals you will gain new business for sure. After reading this article, I see just how important it is to be a guide on how to improve business rather than just a salesman. There is no such thing as just a salesman. We have a responsibility to take care of our customers in every aspect that they see fit. A customer service business consultant is a better title for successful people in sales."

Cullin Hamm

5. How can you appeal to their buying senses?

Keep in mind in considering the appeal to their three senses that you and I, as a sales person, are now back stage. We are manipulating the scenery, the lights and the actors, to produce the effect we want on the audience - our prospect. We are "staging" this show - our presentation - to transport him mentally to an ideal tomorrow. In picking apart the elements of the presentation to find what it is made of, we are making a slow motion picture of a process which in practice often speeds so fast that its parts flow imperceptibly into one another.

Your prospect understands most quickly through his eyes. It is their major sense in perceiving the new, and far stronger than remembering what you say. Most people can visualize in their memory what Niagara Falls looks like, but few can recall the sound of the falls. Hence wherever you can use a sketch, a drawing, a chart, a picture, or a sample you are strengthening what you say a thousand times.

If you have just a little artistic ability, and can pencil your ideas on a scratch pad to the prospect as you talk, it is extremely effective. Planned presentations which are mainly visual need no defense. Visual technique is generally accepted as superior from every standpoint.

Don't neglect their hands. One of the most human reactions is to grab. There is a subconscious feeling of possession when we hold something - and this is the effect you are after - for him or her to picture a future day when they will using what you show them for increased profits. Let him or her handle your product and get the feel of it. Go slowly! They are grasping what you say with difficulty. A person can't take more than one idea at a time.

You're teaching now, and your customer is slowly absorbing your first lesson. Keep the language simple, so even a child can understand. Always assume he or she knows nothing about your product. Even when you repeat what he or she already knows, they like it, because it makes them feel well informed. Your voice should vibrate with enthusiasm - which cannot be faked.

This is a good time to ask reinforcing questions about their positive experience.

If you are cooking a new product for them to sample, take a good wiff of it yourself and then have them do the same.

If you are selling a boat, have them feel the smooth finish and tell them how it will easily glide through the water.

If you are selling a vacation, show them pictures of the fun they are going to have.

Comments:

If I know my sales call is going to be in an office over a desk, I bring lots of pictures. I talk slow and direct, with short imaging sentences, with a little longer pause, letting the client 'see it working in his own mind'.   What is even better is when I can get the client up and back in the area of their business the item is going to be used and start 'painting.   Remember quite time between 'strokes of the brush' is good. And try always to keep the flow of information smooth and easy to understand.

David Vize

Artists have a vision & then use that vision to create an image that others can see & understand. By illustrating their vision it allows the potential viewers to form the same picture or concept they are portraying. In sales it's the same concept; you are painting a picture where the ultimate goal is having the customer see & understand how your product or service will be of benefit to them.

Carla McCrea

I could see where it would be good to paint a picture of our business to a client/customer. You could tell them to imagine their business where they would get the best quality of employees & customer service available, as well as corporate support.

April Swain

I understand the meaning behind this lesson. If someone can touch or see a product they will be more open to the product and the purchasing of it. This may not necessarily work with everything we sell because some services cant be "handled" . But we can pain them a picture of how our service can be of an advantage to them. It may take more imagination but we can put a "picture" in their head.

Brandon Sanchez

Nothing is real until experience it. How often do you purchase a product with out picking it up and examining it from all angles? You usually try on clothes, lie down on a bed or sofa or pick up dishes just to see if they feel right. Usually the less routine the purchase, and the more expensive the item, the more important it is to touch it before buying. This is why our Senses play a very important role in helping our customers understand and interpret their experiences. Our job is to manipulate those senses to our benefit and attract more customers through their own senses so that they can buy from us.

Yessie Narvaez

"In a study done on children, it was proven that the majority retained more knowledge when taught through movement or by taking a physical part in learning. I used this as a teacher and based my lesson plans around this idea."

Angie

6. How can you prepare the customer for your presentation?

Use the first few words of your presentation to prepare the prospect for what they are about to see.

Lets look at your presentation as you unfold it step by step, from another angle, that part which should come first. A presentation is like any good show. The opening of the first act must be unusually good or your audience will walk out before you get underway. And the first few lines of any play are used by the writer to prepare the way for the action which follows. Therefore the first few words should fit the prospect with a pair of "spectacles" so that he will see what you later display.

You might say, for example, "now I am going to show you the new marketing program which will begin next month". Before I take it out of my brief case I want you to bear in mind that a good marketing plan is one which moves, which has brilliant color, which carries a headline to stop the customer." Then when you bring out your new program, you force him to see it through "spectacles" of your own making, enhancing its value to him.

Never dump a sample, or a prospectus, into his or her lap without first preparing his mind to see what it is. Even a monthly flier should not be shown without first holding it back for a moment until you explain what you are going to show. This move brings into play one of the strongest of his mental attributes ...Curiosity.

Your presentation should be looked upon as a good teaching job. Keep technical terms and discussions out. Don't describe how it is made, what it is made of, what its construction advantages are over a competitor's... unless you do so in terms of what these advantages will mean to the buyer when he uses it. You cannot transport the prospect to this better tomorrow until he or she understands what you are selling. Hence the next step in your presentation is a straight forward teaching job, simply one of downright instruction which must be finished before you can talk about the value of your merchandise.

In going through a prospect's ear to the seat of his imagination in order to help him "take off" to an ideal "tomorrow", you should use all of the known principles of effective speech. Keep the voice low, modulated, which conveys the impression of reserve power and gives casual emphasis to important points when you raise your voice.

The finest check you can use to avoid making this common mistake is to keep in mind constantly your objective, to build a picture of the prospect - seeing him or her using your product. No one is interested in the exact mixture of a product, or the percentage of this or that ingredient, unless they view it from the standpoint of how it will be a benefit, making more money and bringing in more customers.

Here is a good example: I got on the plane and just as I settled in, the woman next to me asked where I was from. I told her, trying not to encourage a conversation.

She not only told me where she was from, she volunteered that she had brain surgery – twice! I tried to look interested but I was tired. She kept going on and on and the next thing I knew, I fell asleep while she was talking.

It was a good reminder on how our customers feel most of the time. Sales people call on their customers and talk about their "brain surgery" while the customer has a hundred things on their mind and a hundred things to do.

What is the solution? How do we get our customers to listen?

Pinpoint relevancy: asking well thought out questions to find out what future pictures your customer has in their mind, and then positioning your product or service with surgical precision to help turn those pictures into reality.

Here's how David Vize, a real sales pro and friend of mine, describes it:

"One thing I learned over the years is the most powerful tool to use in a presentation is the customer's own words or their own understanding of what they wanted. At the point of giving a presentation I will have already gathered all the needed information.   I start my presentation with,

"Early on you told me…"

 "Now I want to make sure I understood you to say…"

"You told me you wanted to achieve…"

"I will use their name in place of the word, you.   "Mr. Smith, early on you told me…."

"Using the person name will wake them up to you a little, and using their own words will tie them to your presentation."

"It's easy to say no to you or to your offering but it's hard for one to say 'No' to what their own words have said. "

Selling isn't brain surgery, or is it? Selling is psychological brain surgery and pinpoint relevancy is when the sales person asks specific questions about what the prospect is interested in.

If the woman sitting next to me on the plane would have asked me a few questions and used my answers to set the stage for her "brain surgery," I would have felt more engaged and would not have fallen asleep.

However, "where are you from let me tell you about my double brain surgery" just didn't cut it.

The key lesson is simple - engage and set the stage before you tell your story.

Comments:

The best way to prep a customer is to call them to let them know you are coming and let them know you are going to be talking about x, y or z. Let them know you have the stuff you said you would. This will give the operator time to warm himself up and sell himself on his own ideas. By the time you get there they are ready to go, excited and have questions for you to go over.

Dave Ferren

The best way to prepare your customer is to first let them know you are coming. I had one of my biggest presentations to date, and I had forgotten to call him. When we arrived he was on his way out the door to a doctor's appointment, and only a couple minutes for to me to talk about our services. Although, it still went well, we did not get the entire message across. So always be prepared on your end before attempting to prepare your customer.

Jason Kirouac

Being able to make the customer "see" how you can help them become more efficient and effective is a good way to prepare them for the presentation. I emphasize on the features I offer that will ultimately make their life "easier".

Brooke Knight

I think a good way to a great presentation to a future client/customer, is show them in detail, of what your company is capable of & what we do. As well as using bold colors & words to entice them so you catch their attention.

April Swain

This approach is similar to movies. At the beginning they begin to set you up slowly & get you excited & curious about what is fixing to come. Taking it one step at a time & then showing excitement for the conclusion builds their anticipation & curiosity so once the grand finale is presented they are just as excited about the product or service as you are.

Carla McCrea

A good presentation is like a great menu. A great menu has a menu cover has to attract your attention and WANT you to open the menu to order the product! Once the menu is open, the waiter/waitress (salesperson) must guide them through the menu to relive the customers hunger and thirst. AND do not forget about dessert! This is a classic example of first and last impression but with great thoughts, ideas, products and services in the middle.

Roland DeGregorio

I really like the concept of selling by using senses. We have a very colorful sheet that lists our 57 solutions by columns which is a great selling tool for our payroll services. (I ran out one time and had to make photocopies and that was not impressive) We use a colorful folder to display our brochures. The only thing I put in front of the customer is our 57 solutions sheet. This is a good way for the customer to follow me when I am explaining what this service covers. I pull my chair right up beside them and point things out as I am talking and answering their questions. I want to be on their level and almost look at it, as if for the first time myself and display my excitement about what this service covers. Thank you for your other hints regarding the senses. This will help me a lot.

Patsy Clements,

7. How can the customer do the closing?

When a customer has made up their mind that they are going to buy, they buy, they do the closing.

From time to time you should try to discover just how much you have accomplished in transporting the person in front of you to a state where he or she sees themselves using what you have to offer to their advantage. This can be done with "qualifiers" put in the form of questions such as, "where do you plan to put this, Mr. Brown?"

The psychology of the "close" has been so talked about by sales experts that it has frightened more sales people than it has helped. When a person has made up their mind that they are going to make their imaginary picture a reality, then they do the closing, they buy, you don't sell them except to make it easy for them to sign an order.

You started to close the moment you decided to call for the appointment. You are closing all the way through the process.

This magical key has infinite possibilities. It automatically solves the question of trying to make a complete presentation while the prospect is being constantly interrupted. When he finds himself - in his imagination - in tomorrow, he himself handles the job of shutting out interruptions. He, more than you, refuses to let anyone else spoil his "picture." He will tell the person at the switchboard to stop all telephone calls to his office for an hour, or ask someone else to wait on customers.

As your presentation proceeds it should include steps which apparently fit into the running story but which actually are used by you to anticipate objections. The time to answer most objections is before they are brought up, during the presentation.

Here is the TRUTH about closing...

If you don't build rapport YOU WILL NEVER CLOSE

If you don't get them talking YOU WILL NEVER CLOSE

If you don't gain their trust YOU WILL NEVER CLOSE

If you don't make a great presentation YOU WILL NEVER CLOSE

If you don't overcome their objections YOU WILL NEVER CLOSE

If you don't make it easy for them to buy YOU WILL NEVER CLOSE

If you don't fit your product into their future YOU WILL NEVER CLOSE

If you don't follow up on your promises YOU WILL NEVER CLOSE

If you don't ask for the order YOU WILL NEVER CLOSE

Usually people who have never had to go out and ACTUALLY MAKE A SALE think that selling is all about closing. Trying too hard to close without providing the rest of the program will turn off customers faster than anything else you do...

Comments:

Each of the TURTH in closing must be done, or you will never close, but if I may, I would like to add one more that I believe would fall at the end of the list,

If you don't recognize that it's been sold YOU WILL NEVER CLOSE

We work so hard to get to the close, we have more 'Yes's' than 'No's' but for some reason we fear that closing 'No' - it seems so final that we keep right on selling.

I had a manager call me up and tell me about this new salesman he has hired about eight months ago, "He is a great kid, got the talent, but I just can't get the closing numbers out of him. Could you find some time and work with him and see if you can see what I'm missing to help this young man sell more." Well, I have never seen so many 'prospect's' eyes light up when Jerry stopped by to call on them. As one prospect told me, Jerrys a great guy, has really helped me out.... But he has never ask for an order.

David Vize

Closing a deal is difficult because a deal is never really closed. When we ask or receive an order that's not the close of a deal that's the end of the sell and the beginning of the relationship. If a deal is truly closed then there will be no more deals which mean no more orders. We want to keep the deal open and continue to service the client and be the go to source for all their needs. If we think a deal is closed because they place an order we are very wrong, that would be the same as if we went to a restaurant placed our order and the waiter or waitress didn't come back, they got the order so why would they need to follow up. Because its never closed.

Brandon Sanchez

This article does a good job explaining how to "close." Closing is not simply done at the end of a sale. It is an ongoing job. I like to think that my job with a customer is

never done. The deal with a customer is never complete.
Years of taking care of the customer in every way possible
is still considered to be part of closing. I never want to take
my clients for granted. The minute I slip up, they will move
on to a "better deal."

Cullin Hamm

"This is so refreshing to hear. I had to sit through a sales
training seminar where we had to come up with ten closes.
I could feel the tension in the room as we all tried to
rehearse the prepared closes that everyone knows,
including the customer, and few really use."

Mickey

Well this is one of the most important lessons and I have
been waiting on it. Everyone has talked to me about
closing. I have received information and guidance from my
RVP, my VP and my Coach. Everyone has their own little
style or way of telling me how to close. I truly guess that
there is no certain way (set in stone) that a person closes.
I have closed on the very first trip to the customer and
walked out with a signed agreement and a work order. I
have closed after spending 6 months stopping by every

other week and leaving a pad and pen. I have been told that I have their business and the customer so much as telling me they are going to sign, but just not right then due to what ever circumstances they may be going through at that time. To be honest, I am not sure if I have developed "my style" for closing. It seems to me that it just happens in a natural way. Some sales calls I have been on last 5 to 10 minutes and some have lasted over 2 hours. It sort of depends on the customer and how much "they" want to talk. I have learned that the more they talk, the more you can find out what their "needs really are."

 My "Coach" has told me on several of our many talks that "I need to stop talking" as soon as the customer tells you he wants to buy your product. He told me the selling is complete and the next step is the order and the paperwork. He told me you do not have to keep selling. I believe that this is some of the best information I have ever received. As far as the 9 "if you don't" areas go, I hope that I am practicing them faithfully with all of my customers. This is an area I will go back and examine just to be sure and be on the safe side.

Patsy Clements, Sales Manager

About the author Bob Oros

Regardless of whether you are reading one of his books or attending one of his programs, the most frequent comment is: "This guy has been there, he is one of us, I am going to use these strategies."

With over 2,000 speaking engagements in all 50 states and several international locations for manufacturers, distributors and associations, you can be sure you will get the results and information you are looking for. Prior to starting his speaking career, Bob served six years in the US Navy as a Communications Specialist and then worked his way from a street sales person to the position of National Sales Manager for a Fortune 200 company.

Bob has received awards for speaking, writing and marketing too numerous to mention.

Additional Topics by Bob Oros

Why Sales People Fail

The Key to Selling Anybody

The Power of Expectations

Add Value to Every Product

How to Justify Your Price

Lost in 60 Seconds

One Good Reason to Buy

Control a Buyer's Attitude

How to Create Demand

Smoke Screen Objections

Take the Risk Out of Sales

How Small Companies Get Big

Small Companies Get Big

www.ingramcontent.com/pod-product-compliance
Lightning Source LLC
Chambersburg PA
CBHW021926170526
45157CB00005B/2203